GIL KREITER

How to Collect a Judgment

You've Won Your Lawsuit, Now Get the Money You Are Owed

Copyright © 2024 by Gil Kreiter

All rights reserved. No part of this publication may be reproduced, stored or transmitted in any form or by any means, electronic, mechanical, photocopying, recording, scanning, or otherwise without written permission from the publisher. It is illegal to copy this book, post it to a website, or distribute it by any other means without permission.

Gil Kreiter asserts the moral right to be identified as the author of this work.

Gil Kreiter has no responsibility for the persistence or accuracy of URLs for external or third-party Internet Websites referred to in this publication and does not guarantee that any content on such Websites is, or will remain, accurate or appropriate.

Designations used by companies to distinguish their products are often claimed as trademarks. All brand names and product names used in this book and on its cover are trade names, service marks, trademarks and registered trademarks of their respective owners. The publishers and the book are not associated with any product or vendor mentioned in this book. None of the companies referenced within the book have endorsed the book.

First edition

This book was professionally typeset on Reedsy.
Find out more at reedsy.com

Contents

1	Introduction	1
2	Collecting Information	3
3	Ivanka Trump Collection	11
4	Sam's Wife's Business	12
5	Moving a Judgment to a New State	13
6	Conclusion	15
7	Resource - Information Subpoena	16
8	Resource - Income Execution	21
9	Resource - Info Subpoena with Restraining Notice	28

1

Introduction

Congratulations! You've won your case! Whether you are an attorney, or a collection agency, or a debt buyer, or a landlord, or an individual, you now have to collect your money. It might have taken a year or more for the court to award you the judgment. There were many appearances, lots of papers to file, you had to pay process servers and court fees. You spent time and or money getting this judgment.Time now for the payback.

The court will not help you, the county sheriff will serve papers for you, but no one will tell you what to do next. What now?

About You

You are a collection attorney paid on contingency. If you don't find the money, you have wasted your time. You won't get paid.

Or you are a collection agency also paid on contingency as above.

Or you are a debt buyer who has spent money buying the debt and on the lawsuit.

Or you are the creditor.Most painful of all, you have lost the money and you want to get it back. You are entitled to it.

About Us

We have been collecting judgments since 2009. That is the only thing that we do. I will explain everything that we do and how we do it so that you have a better chance of getting your money (or your client's money) back. After all, you didn't go to court for fun, but rather, to get your money back.

Let's get to work!

2

Collecting Information

What the creditor knows

The creditor, call him Charlie, had some sort of relationship to the debtor, call him Dan. That's how this started. Charlie lent Dan money to buy a used car dealership, or to buy a house to renovate and flip. They were friends at one point, and they still might know people in common. Charlie might have gotten one or more checks from Dan in partial payment. That is a good starting point. The idea is to get an idea of what Dan is doing these days and use that knowledge to find his assets, since he isn't voluntarily paying Charlie back.

Credit report

We pull a credit report on Dan. That gives us information on where he is living now, and what his bills are and who he is paying. Here is the first section of the credit report:

TRANSUNION TRUVISION CREDIT REPORT

\<FOR\> \<SUB NAME\> \<MKT SUB\> \<INFILE\> \<DATE\> \<TIME\>
(I) Z AM7668471 MICROBILT 13 ER 7/88 10/02/23 09:11CT

HOW TO COLLECT A JUDGMENT

```
<SUBJECT><SSN> <BIRTH DATE>
   XXXXXX, DAN XXX-XX-1066 10/53
   <ALSO KNOWN AS>
   XXXXXX,DAN
   XXXXXX,DAN, NELSON
   NELSONXXXXXX,DAN
   <CURRENT ADDRESS><DATE RPTD>
   6 HOFFMAN AV., XXX CITY PA. 16301 9/95
   <FORMER ADDRESS>
   14 W. FRONT ST., XXX CITY PA. 16301 12/90
   <POSITION>
   <CURRENT EMPLOYER AND ADDRESS> <VERF> <RPTD>
   NC PLASTIC COMPANY RETIRED LABORER
   10/16A 9/16
   <FORMER EMPLOYER AND ADDRESS>
   RETIRED RETIRED
   OIL CITY PA.11/15
```

The report is on Dan XXXXX with the social security number (redacted) and date of birth on the first line. Following is his current address, and former address, there is often more than one former address. The current employer is usually out of date, but can give you an idea of what kind of job he may have.

The next section has details of Dan's economic life:

TRADES
   SUBNAMESUBCODE OPENED HIGHCRED TERMS MAXDELQPAYPAT
1-12 MOP

COLLECTING INFORMATION

ACCOUNT# VERFIED CREDLIM PASTDUEAMT-MOP PAYPAT 13-24 ECOA COLLATRL/LOANTYPE CLSD/PD BALANCE REMARKS MO 30/60/90

MARINR FINCF 2EN4001 9/16 $3191036MI09
780301320113 8/23A $31
CSECURED 4/20F $31UNPAID BLNC CHRGD OFF 0

The charged off accounts won't help, so ignore these.

```
TRUMARK FIN   Q 6950001  9/17   $1000      MIN25
111111111111 R01
434575001034            9/23A  $1000     $0
111111111111
I    CREDIT CARD               $908
                          48   0/ 0/ 0


MEMBERS 1ST   Q 6755004  9/23   $52.6K    084M812
                         I01
12451280001              9/23A            $0
I    AUTOMOBILE                 $52.6K
                          0


FREEDOM MTG   F 2C82001  10/14  $78.5K    360M918
111111111111 M01
89645006                 8/23A            $0
111111111111
I    FHA R.E. MORTGAGE          $65.6K
```

```
                        48    1/ 0/ 0

SANTANDER BK B 468S036  8/10   $1044    MIN27
111111111111 C01
617401453960            8/23A  $1000    $0
111111111111
    I    LINE OF CREDIT        $916
                        48    0/ 0/ 0
```

In the above four accounts is where the gold is. No guarantees, but here is where you have the best chances to find useful information.

Dan is paying his Trumark Financial credit card very regularly, that is the meaning of the 1s on the right, he is paying on time. So you can request information on how Dan is paying from Trumark, what bank he is using to make the last 5 payments, say, by sending them a subpoena. The resources section has a copy of the subpoena we use.

He has a car loan with Members 1st Bank. At the time I pulled this report he hadn't made a payment yet. So you can wait a month to subpoena them. But because this is such a new loan, the work information the bank has will be current. That could be the home run on this report.

Dan also owns property, he has a mortgage that is serviced by Freedom Mortgage. You can subpoena them for the property information, and the payment information also.

He has a line of credit with Santander Bank, N.A. same questions to them. That is, how does Dan pay and what secures the line of credit. Maybe he has a hunting cabin that was paid for by the line of credit.

COLLECTING INFORMATION

WEBBNK/FHUTD 2CSN002 6/15 $0 111111111111 R01
636992104743 2/18A $1000$0 111111111111
ICHARGE ACCOUNT 1/18C $0CLOSED 32 0/ 0/ 0

REG FINF 3645005 11/15 $3780 036M 111111111 I01
50721001 9/16A $0
CUNSECURED 9/16C $0CLOSED 10 0/ 0/ 0

REG FINF 3645005 3/15 $3410036M 11111111 I01
50693601 11/15A $0
CUNSECURED 11/15C $0CLOSED 8 0/ 0/ 0

CAPITAL ONEB 1DTV001 9/13 $0 111111111111 R01
517805944027 8/15A $300$0 1111111111
ICREDIT CARD 7/15C $0CLSD BY CRDT GRANTOR 22 0/ 0/ 0

REG FINF 3645005 3/15 $1798036MI01
50692601 3/15A $0
IUNSECURED 3/15C $0CLOSED 0

GALAXY FCUQ 236Y005 8/11 $4099060M 111111111111 I01
114716E 1/15A $0 1111111111
CUNSECURED 1/15C $0CLOSED 40 0/ 0/ 0

T R U V I S I O N C R E D I T R E P O R T S E R V I C E D B Y :
TRANSUNION 800-888-4213
2 BALDWIN PLACE, P.O. BOX 1000 CHESTER, PA 19016
CONSUMER DISCLOSURES CAN BE OBTAINED ONLINE THROUGH TRANSUNION AT:
HTTP://WWW.TRANSUNION.COM

END OF TRANSUNION REPORT

The closed accounts won't help, so ignore these.

TheWorkNumber

One of the credit reporting agencies, Equifax, owns a business that allows you to enter a social security number, and if the employer reports to The Work Number, returns the employer and when the employee started work and their current address and phone number (sometimes). This is a great shortcut for creditors in states where you can garnish wages.

This is great for debt buyers who can query The Work Number database once a year and get some hits that can then be sent to their lawyer to prepare an income execution. There is a NY State income execution in the Resources section at the end of the book. The income execution is then sent to a county sheriff to serve first on the debtor-employee, then, if after 21 days he doesn't pay voluntarily, the income execution is served on the debtor's employer. The employer has to withhold 10% of the employee's wages to pay down the judgment.

I once had a tenant who was an undercover narcotics cop. He got tired of making small buys on the street and decided to retire early. He had nowhere near 20 years on the job to retire, so he shot himself in the leg so that he could retire on disability.

He owed me rent, so after I got the judgment I filed an income execution and got in line with everyone else he owed money to. Luckily my judgment was paid before he retired.

Which brings up an important point. Pensions, social security, unemployment payments cannot be garnished.

Property Search

COLLECTING INFORMATION

Most counties have their property records searchable online. Usually, you can put in the name of the debtor and see if he owns any property. Not all first mortgages are listed on the credit report, and he may own the property free and clear. So we always search county records for property and get copies of deeds and mortgages. Here again, the mortgage company can be subpoenaed for information on how Dan pays his mortgage.

We have a client, Denise, who slipped and hurt herself in front of Neville and Merle's house. They didn't have homeowner's insurance so they had to defend themselves in court. They lost but couldn't pay the judgment. We found out, by searching the property records, that they owned an investment property. We agreed, with Denise's consent, that they could sell the property and pay off the judgment. They had to get a tenant out to make the property saleable, so we waited. After 9 months, we found out that they changed their mind and deeded the houses to a trust. Very bad behavior!

So we filed in court to reverse the sale as a fraudulent conveyance. By deeding their home and investment properties to a trust, they made themselves insolvent. They have agreed to sell the investment property to pay off the judgment after all.

For another client, we started collecting the rent in a building owned by the judgment debtor. That brought in a few thousand dollars a month. I had to repair issues in the apartments and generally act as the landlord. We sold our clients lien on the property for $100,000.

For an extended family that won a judgment against a brokerage and the owner of the defuct brokerage, we filed a motion to reverse a transfer of the debtor's condo to a trust. The judge has since sided with us and reversed the transfer, and we have filed a property execution with the Sheriff to sell the condo at auction to pay off the judgment.

The judge insisted that we personally serve a copy of the ruling on the debtor. The process server went to the condo, and the people working there told him that the debtor did own the condo, but didn't live there. So I thought that maybe he was back living with his ex-wife.

She had sold their house in Purchase and bought an apartment in nearby White Plains. Sure enough, when the process server visited the wife's apartment, she reached the debtor by phone from the lobby, but he wouldn't let her up to receive the papers. She had to leave them downstairs with the concierge and mail a copy.

A week later, we heard from the debtor's lawyer. The lawyer tried to stop the sale of his condo, but the judge pushed everyone to settle on a payment plan. We got the first check for $80,000.00 and, in later months, all the payments of the payment plan.

Bank Searches

If the targeted search using the credit report doesn't yield a bank for the debtor, one can subpoena the banks. As of 2023, JPMorgan Chase holds approximately 16% of all bank deposits in the US. Bank of America holds almost 15%; Wells Fargo holds almost 11%; Citibank holds almost 6%; U.S. Bank holds almost 3.5%. Just these banks together hold approximately 51.5% of all bank deposits in the country. If you add in the next ten banks, the fifteen banks together hold over 76% of all bank deposits.

For debt buyers with many debtors to work with at once, the banks allow bulk subpoenas where you send a file of all the debtors and the bank returns a list of hits, which debtors have accounts with them

Once you have found the bank, you can freeze the bank account. If there is not enough in the bank to pay the judgment in full, you can subpoena the bank for the last six months of bank statements so that we can see where debtor's income is coming from.

3

Ivanka Trump Collection

Before Ivanka Trunp and her husband saved the world as part of her father's presidential administration, she designed and licensed her name for a jewelry line. Her partner, an experienced New York City jeweler, contracted with a large manufacturer based in Hong Kong to make the jewelry. The Ivanka Trump Collection owed the manufacturer three million dollars, so the manufacturer hired me to collect the judgment. By the way, the retailer also owes Ivanka $200,000.

To get a partial payment to the manufacturer we prepared a property execution against Neiman Marcus to turn over all the Ivanka Trump jewelry they had in all their stores to the NYC marshal that we work with. Neiman Marcus sent us the jewelry and we held an auction to reimburse the manufacturer.

4

Sam's Wife's Business

One of our clients, David, lent Sam a million dollars for a used car dealership on Long Island. At the time of the judgment, Sam still owed David almost $900,000.

David hired us to recover his judgment. We didn't find any bank accounts for Sam, but we did find accounts for his wife. We froze those accounts, claiming that Sam was operating through his wife. Once the accounts were frozen, Sam was willing to negotiate a payment plan to pay David back. He sends us a $7,500 check every month.

5

Moving a Judgment to a New State

Couple: Hey fellas, that's our car.
Men: You shouldn't park here in front of the club.
Couple: Why not? It's a legal spot.
Men: A**holes, you are blocking the entrance to the club.
Couple: There is no need for foul language!
Men: Shut the f** up, b**ch!
Man in couple: Don't talk to her like that!
Men: F** you.

The three thugs beat up the couple, David and Mandy (names changed to protect their privacy).

David and Mandy filed suit in the Superior Court of the Virgin Islands, Division of St. Thomas & St. John. They won two separate judgments, David for $64,475.00 and Mandy for $175,970.50.

Seven years later, they had received nothing.

Then Mandy hired us to collect her judgment. I found the former owner of the club—one of the assailants—in Henderson Nevada, and located a second, one of his security thugs, in Miami. The third, a suspended policeman, still lives in the Virgin Islands. I moved the case, legally called domesticating the judgment in the new jurisdiction, to Nevada and, using the judgment as legal cause, froze their bank accounts. We domesticated the judgment in Florida as well and froze the ex-club security man's account.

6

Conclusion

Your judgment is a powerful tool to recover the money that you have lost. You can use it creatively to find the debtor's assets and get your money back. If you have any comments or questions, email me at Gil@BloomingdalePartners.com.

Resource - Information Subpoena

Supreme Court of the State of New York
County of Ulster

---X

High Flow Funding LLC		
Judgment Creditor,		Index No. EF2021-1066
-against-		**INFORMATION SUBPOENA**
Aaron BBBBBB (SSN: XXX-XX-XXXX) d/b/a		
Aaron BBBBBB Construction,		
Judgment Debtor(s).		

---X

THE PEOPLE OF THE State of New York TO: Santander Consumer USA, Inc.
c/o CT Corporation System
Legal Order Processing
28 Liberty Street, 42nd Floor
New York, NY 10005.

GREETING: Whereas, in an action in SUPREME Court, County of Ulster, between High Flow Funding LLC as plaintiff and Aaron BBBBBB d/b/a Aaron BBBBBB Construction as defendant(s), who are all the parties named in said action, a judgment was entered on 16th day of August, 2021 in favor of High Flow Funding LLC, plaintiff and against Aaron BBBBBB d/b/a Aaron BBBBBB Construction, defendant(s), in the amount of $92,638.52 of which $92,638.52 together with interest thereon from 16th day of August, 2021 remains due and unpaid.

NOW THEREFORE WE COMMAND YOU, that you answer in writing under oath, separately and fully, each question in the questionnaire accompanying this subpoena, each answer referring to the question to which it responds; produce each and every document requested, and that you return the answers and documents together with the original questions **within 7 days** after your receipt of the subpoena and attached questions.

TAKE NOTICE that false swearing or failure to comply with this subpoena is punishable as a contempt of court.

I HEREBY CERTIFY THAT THIS SUBPOENA COMPLIES WITH RULE 5224 OF THE CIVIL PRACTICE LAW AND RULES AND SECTION 601 OF THE GENERAL BUSINESS LAW, THAT I HAVE A REASONABLE BELIEF THAT THE PARTY RECEIVING THIS SUBPOENA HAS IN THEIR POSSESSION INFORMATION ABOUT THE DEBTOR THAT WILL ASSIST THE CREDITOR IN COLLECTING THE JUDGMENT.

DATED: March 27, 2024

_____, Esq.
Attorney for the Plaintiff
Reply to: BRR, LLC
157 East 106th Street, #8
New York, NY 10029
Gil@BloomingdalePartners.com
(718) 360 -1354 voice
(718) 788 -0859 facsimile

QUESTIONS AND ANSWERS FOR INFORMATION SUBPOENA

STATE OF _____ COUNTY OF _____)

_____ being duly sworn deposes and says: deponent is the _____ of Santander Consumer USA, Inc. c/o CT Corporation System. ("you" or "your") recipient of an information subpoena herein and the original and a copy of the questions and requests accompanying said subpoena. The answers set forth below are made from information obtained from the records of the recipient. All references to judgment debtor refer to Aaron BBBBBB d/b/a Aaron BBBBBB Construction. All references to judgment creditor refer to High Flow Funding LLC. If necessary, please attach additional sheet of paper to these responses in order to provide complete answers to every question.

Q1: Please list from your records for each account held by each defendant:

Name of account holder:

Type of account:

Address of account holder:

phone number of account holder:

date of birth of account holder:

tax ID of account holder:

balance of account:

Q2: For each CREDIT or LOAN account of Aaron BBBBBB d/b/a Aaron BBBBBB Construction please list the last five payments made on the account:

Date	Amount	ABA Routing Number of Source
1)_____	_____	_____
2)_____	_____	_____
3)_____	_____	_____

4) _____ _____ _____

5) _____ _____ _____

Q3: For each DEPOSITORY account of Aaron BBBBBB d/b/a Aaron BBBBBB Construction please list the last five payments/transfers made from the account:

    Date   Amount   Destination

1) _____ _____ _____

2) _____ _____ _____

3) _____ _____ _____

4) _____ _____ _____

5) _____ _____ _____

Q4: For each DEPOSITORY account of Aaron BBBBBB d/b/a Aaron BBBBBB Construction please list the last five deposits made into the account:

    Date   Amount   Source Name and Address

1) _____ _____ _____

2) _____ _____ _____

3) _____ _____ _____

4)_____   _____   _____

5)_____   _____   _____

Sign Name: _____

Print Name: _____

Sworn to before me this _____ day of _____ 2024.

_____
Notary Public

Please return this form to:

BRR, LLC

157 East 106th Street, #8

New York, NY 10029

Gil@BloomingdalePartners.com

718 360 1354 voice

718 788 0859 facsimile

Resource - Income Execution

SUPREME COURT OF THE STATE OF NEW YORK
COUNTY OF ONONDAGA
---X

High Flow Funding LLC	
Judgment Creditor,	Index No. 001171 / 2021
-against-	**INCOME EXECUTION**
John A. RRRR (SSN: XXX-XX-8273) &	
John A. RRRR d/b/The Next Generation Yard &	
Tree Services a/k/a The Next Generation	
Lawn Care	
Judgment Debtor(s).	

---X

THE PEOPLE OF THE STATE OF NEW YORK TO:
Any Sheriff or New York City Marshal, Greeting:

    WHEREAS, in an action in SUPREME Court, County of ONONDAGA, between High Flow Funding LLC as plaintiff and John A. RRRR & John A. RRRR d/b/The Next Generation Yard & Tree Services a/k/a The Next Generation Lawn Care as defendant(s), who are all the parties named in said action, a judgment was entered on 2nd day of December, 2021 in favor of High Flow Funding LLC, plaintiff and against John A. RRRR & John A. RRRR d/b/The Next Generation Yard & Tree Services a/k/a

The Next Generation Lawn Care, defendant(s), in the amount of $20,155.07 of which $20,155.07 together with interest thereon from 2nd day of December, 2021, remains due and unpaid.

WHEREAS the judgment debtor, John A. RRRR is receiving wages commissions, rents, and income from SECURITAS CRITICAL INFRASTRUCTURE SERVICES, INC. c/o National Registered Agents, Inc., located at 28 Liberty Street, New York, NY 10005.

NOW, THEREFORE, WE COMMAND YOU, to serve a copy of this Income Execution upon the judgment debtor, John A. RRRR, NN South Main Street, CCCCCC, NY 13XXX above named within 20 days after it is delivered to you, or if the judgment debtor shall fail to pay any installments pursuant to this Income Execution as commanded for a peRRRRd of 20 days, then you shall levy upon the money that the judgment debtor is receiving or will receive by serving a copy of this Income Execution, endorsed to indicate the extent to which paid installments have satisfied the judgment herein, upon the above named employer within your county in the manner provided in CPLR §5231(e).

Directions to Judgment Debtor: You are notified and commanded immediately to start paying to the Sheriff or Marshal serving a copy of this Income Execution on you, installments of up to ten percent (10%), but no more than the Federal limits set forth below, of all wages, salary, commissions, overtime earnings, or other irregular compensation received or hereafter to be received from your Employer, and to continue paying such installments until the judgment with interest and the fees and expenses of this Income Execution is fully paid and satisfied, and if you fail to do so within 20 days this Income Execution will be served on your Employer by the Sheriff or Marshal.

Directions to the Employer: You are commanded immediately to withhold and pay to the Sheriff or Marshal serving a copy of this Income Execution on you, installments of up to ten percent (10%), but no more than the Federal limits set forth below, of all wages, salary, commissions, overtime earnings, or other irregular compensation now or hereafter coming due to the Judgment Debtor, and to continue paying such installments until the judgment with interest and the fees and expenses of this Income Execution is fully paid and satisfied.

DATED: April 15, 2024

_____, Esq.
Attorney for the Plaintiff
157 East 106th Street, #8
New York, NY 10029
(347) 922-5871 cell
(718) 360 -1354 voice
(718) 788 -0859 facsimile
Gil@BloomingdalePartners.com

This income execution directs the withholding of up to ten percent of the judgment debtor's gross income. In certain cases, however, state or federal law does not permit the withholding of that much of the judgment debtor's gross income. The judgment debtor is referred to New York Civil Practice Law and Rules §5231 and 15 United States Code §1671 et seq.

I. **Limitations on the amount that can be withheld:**
  A. An income execution for installments from a judgment debtor's gross income cannot exceed 10% of the judgment debtor's gross income.
  B. If the judgment debtor's weekly disposable earnings is less than thirty (30) times the greater of the Federal minimum wage ($7.25 per hour or $217.50) or New York State minimum wage (see tables below), no deduction can be made from the judgment debtor's earnings under this income execution.
  C. A judgment debtor's weekly disposable earnings cannot be reduced below the amount arrived at by multiplying 30 hours times the greater of the Federal minimum wage ($7.25 per hour, or $217.50) and New York State minimum wage (see tables below), under this income execution.
  D. If deductions are being made from a judgment debtor's earnings under any order of alimony or child support or maintenance for family members or former spouses, and those deductions equal or exceed 25% of the judgment debtor's disposable earnings, then no deduction can be made from the judgment debtor's earnings under this income execution.
  E. If deductions are being made from a judgment debtor's earnings under any order of alimony or child support or maintenance for family members or former spouses, and those deductions are less than 25% of judgment debtor's disposable earnings, deductions may be made from the judgment debtor's earnings under this income execution. However deductions made from a judgment debtor's earnings under any order of alimony or child support or maintenance for family members or former spouses and deductions made under this income execution cannot exceed 25% of judgment debtor's disposable earnings.

NOTE: Nothing in this notice limits the proportion or amount which may be deducted under any order for alimony, support, or maintenance for family members or former spouses.

II. **Explanation of limitations**
Definitions
Disposable Earnings – Disposable earnings are that part of an individual's earnings left after deducting those amounts that are required by law to be withheld (for example, taxes, social security, and unemployment insurance, but not deductions for union dues, insurance plans, etc.).
Gross Income – Gross income is salary, wages, or other income, including any and all overtime earnings, commissions, and income from trusts, before any deductions are made from such income.

ILLUSTRATIONS REGARDING EARNINGS:

IF DISPOSABLE EARNINGS IS:	AMOUNT TO PAY OR DEDUCT FROM EARNINGS UNDER THIS INCOME EXECUTION IS:
(a) 30 Times the greater of the Federal Minimum Wage ($217.50) or New York State minimum wage (see tables below); OR LESS	No payment of deduction allowed
(b) More than 30 times the **greater** of Federal Minimum Wage ($217.50) or New York State minimum wage (see tables below), and less than 40 times the greater of Federal Minimum Wage ($290.00) or New York State minimum wage (see tables below)	The lesser of: The excess over 30 times the **greater** of Federal Minimum Wage ($217.50) or New York State minimum wage (see tables below) in disposable earnings, or 10% of gross earnings
(c) 40 times the **greater** of Federal Minimum Wage ($290.00) or New York State minimum wage (see tables below) OR MORE	The lesser of: 25% of disposable earnings or 10% of gross earnings.

III Notice: You may be able to challenge this income execution through the procedures provided in CPLR §5231(i) and CPLR §5240.

If you think that the amount of your income being deducted under this income execution exceeds the amount permitted by state or federal law, you should act promptly because the money will be applied to the judgment. If you claim that the amount of your income being deducted under this income execution exceeds the amount permitted by state or federal law, you should contact your employer or other person paying your income. Further, YOU MAY CONSULT AN ATTORNEY, INCLUDING LEGAL AID IF YOU QUALIFY. New York State law provides two procedures through which an income execution can be challenged.

CPLR §5231(i) Modification. At any time, the judgment debtor may make a motion to a court for an order modifying an income execution.

CPLR §5240 Modification or protective order: supervision of enforcement. At any time, the judgment debtor may make a motion to a court for an order denying, limiting, conditioning, regulating, extending or modifying the use of any post-judgment enforcement procedure, including the use of income executions.
NOTICE (*CPLR §5230 property execution notice may be technically required by CPLR §5231(a)*)

Pursuant to CPLR §5205(1), $3,425 of an account containing direct deposit or electronic payments reasonably identifiable as statutorily exempt payments, as defined in CPLR §5205(1)(2) is exempt from execution and the garnishee cannot levy upon or restrain $3,425 in such an account.

Pursuant to CPLR §5222(1) an execution shall not apply to an amount equal to, or less than, 90% of the greater of 240 times the federal hourly minimum wage prescribed in the Fair Labor Standards Act of 1938, or 240 times the state hourly minimum wage prescribed in the Labor Law §652 as in effect at the time the earnings are payable, except such part as a court determines to be unnecessary for the reasonable requirements of the judgment debtor and his or her dependents.

NEW YORK STATE MINIMUM WAGES

As of January 1, 2024 the minimum wage in:

New York City, Nassau, Suffolk, and Westchester counties became $16 per hour,
30 times the minimum wage = $480;
40 times the minimum wage = $640.

The rest of New York State, became $15 per hour,
30 times the minimum wage = $450;
40 times the minimum wage = $600.

Resource - Information Subpoena with Restraining Notice

«Court» Court of the «Court_Jurisdiction»
County of «County»

---X

«Plaintiff»	
Judgment Creditor,	Index No. «Index_No»
-against-	**INFORMATION SUBPOENA**
	WITH RESTRAINING NOTICE
«Defendant_1» (SSN: «SSN1»),	
«Defendant_2» (SSN: «SSN2»),	
«Defendant_3» (SSN: «SSN3»)&	
«Defendant_4» (SSN: «SSN4»)	
Judgment Debtor(s).	

---X

      THE PEOPLE OF THE «Court_Jurisdiction» TO: «Bank»
                                                            «Bank_Dept»
                                                            «Bank_Address»
                                                            «Bank_City», «Bank_State»
                                                       «Bank_Zip».

      GREETING: Whereas, in an action in «Court» Court, County of «County», between «Plaintiff» as plaintiff and «Defendant_1» & «Defendant_2» as defendant(s), who are all the parties named in said action, a judgment was entered on «Judgment_Date» in favor of «Plaintiff», plaintiff and against

«Defendant_1» & «Defendant_2», defendant(s), in the amount of «Judgment_Amount» of which «Judgment_Amount» together with interest thereon from «Judgment_Date» remains due and unpaid.

NOW THEREFORE WE COMMAND YOU, that you answer in writing under oath, separately and fully, each question in the questionnaire accompanying this subpoena, each answer referring to the question to which it responds; produce each and every document requested, and that you return the answers and documents together with the original questions **within 7 days** after your receipt of the subpoena and attached questions.

TAKE NOTICE that false swearing or failure to comply with this subpoena is punishable as a contempt of court.

I HEREBY CERTIFY THAT THIS SUBPOENA COMPLIES WITH RULE 5224 OF THE CIVIL PRACTICE LAW AND RULES AND SECTION 601 OF THE GENERAL BUSINESS LAW, THAT I HAVE A REASONABLE BELIEF THAT THE PARTY RECEIVING THIS SUBPOENA HAS IN THEIR POSSESSION INFORMATION ABOUT THE DEBTOR THAT WILL ASSIST THE CREDITOR IN COLLECTING THE JUDGMENT.

RESTRAINING NOTICE

WHEREAS it appears that you are in custody of property in which the judgment debtor has an interest consisting of monies deposited in checking accounts, savings accounts, and or certificates of deposit or other instruments or securities.

TAKE NOTICE that pursuant to CPLR 5222(b) set forth below, you are hereby forbidden to make or suffer any sale, assignment, or transfer of, or any interference with any property that you have an interest, except as provided therein.

TAKE FURTHER NOTICE that this notice also covers all property the judgment debtor has an interest hereafter coming into your custody, and all debts hereafter coming due from you to judgment debtor.

CIVIL PRACTICE LAW AND RULES

Section 5222(b). "Effect of restraint; prohibition of transfer; duration. A judgment debtor or obligor served with a restraining notice is forbidden to make or suffer any sale, assignment, transfer or interference with any property in which he or she has an interest, except upon direction of the sheriff or pursuant to an order of the court, until the judgment or order is satisfied or vacated. A restraining notice served upon a person other than the judgment debtor or obligor is effective only if, at the time of service he or she owes a debt to the judgment debtor or obligor or he or she is in the possession or custody of property in which he or she knows or has reason to believe the judgment debtor or obligor has an interest, or if the judgment creditor or support collection unit has stated in the notice that a specified debt is owed by the person served to the judgment debtor or obligor or that the judgment debtor or obligor has an interest in specified property in the possession or custody of the person served. All property in which the judgment debtor or obligor is known or believed to have an interest therein and thereafter coming into the possession or custody of such a person, including any specified in the notice and all debts of such a person, including any specified in the notice, then due and thereafter coming due to the judgment debtor or obligor, shall be subject to the notice. Such a person is forbidden to make or suffer any sale, assignment or transfer of, or any interference with, any such property, or pay over or otherwise dispose of any such debt, to any person other than the sheriff or the support collection unit, except upon direction of the sheriff or pursuant to any order of the court, until the expiration of one year after the notice is served upon him or her, or until the judgment or order is satisfied or vacated, whichever event first occurs. A judgment creditor or support collection unit which has specified personal property or debt in a restraining notice shall be liable to the owner of the property or the person to whom the debt is owed, if other than the judgment debtor or obligor, for any damages sustained by reason of the restraint. If a garnishee served with a restraining notice withholds the payment of money belonging or owed to the judgment debtor or obligor in an amount equal to twice the amount due on the judgment or order, the restraining notice is not effective a to the other property of money."

TAKE FURTHER NOTICE that disobedience of this Restraining Notice is punishable as a contempt of court.

DATED: November 30, 202__

_____, Esq.
Attorney for the Plaintiff
Reply to:BRR, LLC
301 East 66th Street, #2B
New York, NY 10065
(718) 360 -1354 voice

«Court» Court of the «Court_Jurisdiction»
County of «County»

---X

«Plaintiff»

                Judgment Creditor,   Index No. «Index_No»

         -against-   **INFORMATION SUBPOENA**

                                                         QUESTIONNAIRE

«Defendant_1» (SSN: «SSN1»), «Defendant_2» (SSN: «SSN2»),
& «Defendant_3»(SSN: «SSN3»)

                Judgment Debtor(s).

---X

STATE OF _____)
) ss:
COUNTY OF _____)

_____ being duly sworn deposes and says: deponent is the _____ of «Bank». ("you" or "your") recipient of an information subpoena herein and the original and a copy of the questions and requests accompanying said subpoena. The answers set forth below and the documents and things produced are made from information obtained from the records of the recipient. All references to judgment debtor refer to «Defendant_1». All references to judgment creditor refer to «Plaintiff». If necessary, please attach additional sheet of paper to these responses in order to provide complete answers to every question.

Question Number 1:

Do you have a record of any safe deposit box in which the judgment debtor may have an interest, whether under the name of the judgment debtor, under a trade or corporate name, or in association with others, as of the date of the subpoena or within 1 year pRRRRr thereto?

Answer Number 1:.

Question Number 2:

As to each such safe deposit box, what is the exact designation of the lessees thereof, the date hired, the date discontinued, the names of those having access?

Answer Number 2:

Lessees	Date Hired	Date Discontinued	Those Having Access

Question Number 3:

Do you have possession of any property whatsoever, either real, personal or intangible, including property that may be your collateral, in which the judgment debtor has an interest?

Answer Number 3:

Question Number 4:

What is the description and your estimated value of each item of property responsive to Question No. 3?

Answer Number 4:

Description	Value

Question Number 5:

What do your records show as being the interest of the judgment debtor in each item of property responsive to Question No. 3?

Answer Number 5:

Question Number 6:

Is the judgment debtor indebted to you?

Answer Number 6:

Question Number 7:

As to each indebtedness, what is the amount of the original indebtedness, the date incurred, amount repaid and date of such repayment?

Answer Number 7:

Amount	Date Incurred	Amount Repaid	Date Repaid

Question Number 8:

Do you hold any lien, mortgage, or otherwise, against any property of the judgment debtor?

Answer Number 8:

Question Number 9:

What is the nature of such lien, the full description of the property affected by the lien, the locations and identity of the office of the filing or recording and full indexing information?

Answer Number 9:

Lien	Property	Where Recorded or Filed	Book and Page No.

Question Number 10:

Are you aware of any other transaction with the judgment debtor, either directly or indirectly, as a result of which the judgment debtor may now have, or may in the future become entitled to you for any reason?

Answer Number 10:

Question Number 11:

Has the judgment debtor given you a statement of his or her financial condition?

Answer Number 11:

Question Number 12:

For each of the bank accounts of the judgment debtor's, what is the date that the account was opened, and the amount in the account?

Answer Number 12:

ABA No.   Account No.   Date Opened   Amount in Account

Question Number 13:

For each of the closed bank accounts of the judgment debtor's, what is the date that the account was opened, and the date the account was closed?

Answer Number 13:

ABA No.   Account No.   Date Opened   Date Closed   Amount in Account
                                                        When Closed

Sign Name: _____

Print Name: _____

Position: _____

Name of Financial Institution: _____

Federal Employer Identification No.: _____

Sworn to before me this _____ day of _____ 2020.

_____

Notary Public

Please return this form to:

BRR, LLC

301 East 66th Street, #2B

New York, NY 10065

718 360 1354 voice

718 788 0859 facsimile

«Court» Court of the «Court_Jurisdiction»
County of «County»

---X

«Plaintiff»

              Judgment Creditor,   Index No. «Index_No»

              -against-   **EXEMPTION CLAIM FORM**

«Defendant_1», «Defendant_2» & «Defendant_3»

                  Judgment Debtor(s).

---X

A. , Esq.	B. «Bank»
BRR, LLC	«Bank_Dept»
301 East 66th Street, #2B	«Bank_Address»
New York, NY 10065	«Bank_City», «Bank_State» «Bank_Zip»

Directions: To claim that some or all of the funds in your account are exempt, complete both copies of this form, and make one copy for yourself. Mail or deliver one form to Plaintiff at the address A. and one form to «Bank» at the address B., within twenty days of the date on the envelope holding this notice.

If you have any documents, such as an award letter, an annual statement from your pension, paystubs, copies of checks or bank records showing the last two months of account activity, include copies of the documents with this form. Your account may be released more quickly.

I state that my account contains the following types of funds (check all that apply):

- ☐ Social security
- ☐ Social security disability (SSD)
- ☐ Supplemental security income (SSI)
- ☐ Public assistance

- Wages while receiving SSI of public assistance
- Veterans benefits
- Unemployment insurance
- Income earned in the last 60 days (90% of which is exempt)
- Child support
- Spousal support or maintenance (alimony)
- Workers' compensation
- Railroad retirement or black lung benefits
- Other (describe exemption):
- Payments from pensions and retirement accounts

I request that any correspondence to me regarding my claim be sent to the following address:

Fill in your complete address: _____

_____

I certify under penalty of perjury that the statement above is true to the best of my knowledge and belief.

Date: _____

«Court» Court of the «Court_Jurisdiction»
County of «County»

---X

«Plaintiff»

          Judgment Creditor,   Index No. «Index_No»

          -against-   **EXEMPTION CLAIM FORM**

«Defendant_1», «Defendant_2», & «Defendant_3»

          Judgment Debtor(s).

---X

B. , Esq.	B. «Bank»
BRR, LLC	«Bank_Dept»
301 East 66th Street, #2B	«Bank_Address»
New York, NY 10065	«Bank_City», «Bank_State» «Bank_Zip»

Directions: To claim that some or all of the funds in your account are exempt, complete both copies of this form, and make one copy for yourself. Mail or deliver one form to Plaintiff at the address A. and one form to «Bank» at the address B., within twenty days of the date on the envelope holding this notice.

If you have any documents, such as an award letter, an annual statement from your pension, paystubs, copies of checks or bank records showing the last two months of account activity, include copies of the documents with this form. Your account may be released more quickly.

I state that my account contains the following types of funds (check all that apply):

- ☐ Social security
- ☐ Social security disability (SSD)
- ☐ Supplemental security income (SSI)
- ☐ Public assistance

- Wages while receiving SSI of public assistance
- Veterans benefits
- Unemployment insurance
- Income earned in the last 60 days (90% of which is exempt)
- Child support
- Spousal support or maintenance (alimony)
- Workers' compensation
- Railroad retirement or black lung benefits
- Other (describe exemption):
- Payments from pensions and retirement accounts

I request that any correspondence to me regarding my claim be sent to the following address:

Fill in your complete address: _____

_____

I certify under penalty of perjury that the statement above is true to the best of my knowledge and belief.

Date: _____

www.ingramcontent.com/pod-product-compliance
Lightning Source LLC
Chambersburg PA
CBHW030059230526
45471CB00003B/1166